DATE DUE		

E-MAIL

A TRUE **BOOK**

by
Larry Dane Brimner

Children's Press®

A Division of Grolier Publishing

New York London Hong Kong Sydney
Danbury, Connecticut

Reading Consultant
Linda Cornwell
Learning Resource Consultant
Indiana Department of
Education

For Helen Foster James

Library of Congress Cataloging-in-Publication Data

Brimner, Larry Dane.
    E-Mail / by Larry Dane Brimner.
      p.   cm. — (A true book)
    Includes bibliographical references and index.
    Summary: A simple explanation of what e-mail is and how to use it to
communicate with others through the Internet and the Information
Superhighway.
    ISBN 0-516-20332-0 (lib bdg.)   2SBN 0-516-26168-1 (pbk.)
    1. Electronic mail systems—Juvenile literature. 2. Information super-
highway—Juvenile literature. [1. Electronic mail systems. 2. Internet
(Computer network) 3. Information superhighway.] I. Title. II. Series.
HE6239.E54B75 1997
384.3'4—dc20   96-29053
                                                  CIP
                                                  AC

Contents

Communication isn't always easy.

Communication

People have always sent messages to each other. When they do, it is called communication. The fastest way to communicate is to speak to the other person directly. Sometimes, however, the other person isn't nearby or is busy. How can they communicate then?

People have communicated in many different ways. They have used smoke signals and carrier pigeons. They have sent messages by pony express and telegraph. They have talked

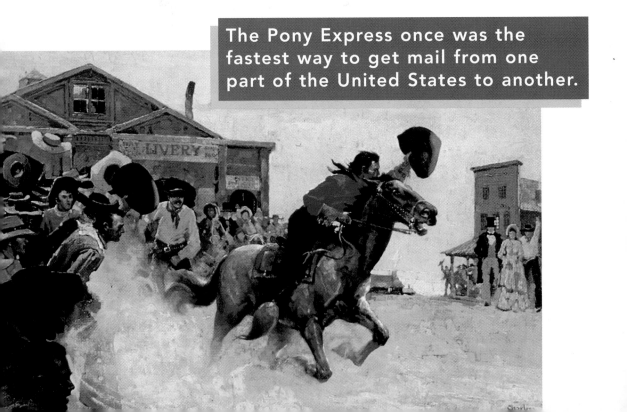

The Pony Express once was the fastest way to get mail from one part of the United States to another.

Now we can call someone
instantly on the phone.

using telephones or, sometimes,
even two cans connected with
a piece of string.

All of these work. But today,
more and more people are
sending messages by electronic
mail, or e-mail.

What Is E-Mail?

E-mail is the fastest way to get a letter from here to there because it uses the "Information Superhighway," or the Internet. The Internet isn't a real highway, of course. It's really a system of computers—a network—connected by telephone lines

Personal computers connect by telephone wires to the Internet, where routers distribute the messages to other computers.

or some other communication path. E-mail is one way to communicate on the Internet. A message written on one computer can be sent to someone else at another computer.

Every person connected to this worldwide computer network has an e-mail address.

E-mail addresses look simple but no two are alike.

someone@anyplace.net

And each person's address is different. If you have a computer on the network, you can send a message to anyone else who has an e-mail address. Your message will get there in a flash, and without paper, an envelope, or a stamp.

Some people think e-mail and the Internet are the same thing. They aren't. E-mail is just one way to use the Internet.

How Does E-Mail Work?

Before you will be able to send or receive e-mail, you will need to outfit your computer correctly. To begin with, you will need a network card or modem. They take the signals from your computer and get messages ready to travel over the Information Superhighway.

To connect to the Internet you will need a modem.

You will also need to subscribe to a service provider that is connected to the Internet. Companies like America Online, CompuServe, and Microsoft Network are used by a lot of people. They provide communication

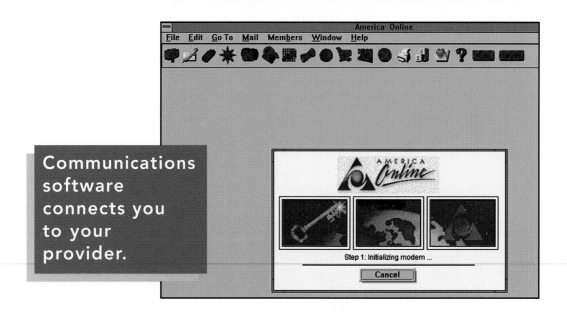

Communications software connects you to your provider.

software to install on your computer. The communication software is what controls your network card or modem.

A service provider owns the host computer that will send and receive your mail. The host computer may also link your computer to other parts of the Internet, like the World Wide Web.

When you send e-mail to a friend, or keypal, the message is broken into small packets of information. The packets are routed over the

The White House

Write to the President of the United States at: president@whitehouse.gov

E-mail can help us keep in touch with our family.

communication lines to your keypal's address. Then they're put back together in the correct order, ready and waiting to be read.

Good News and Bad News

People like e-mail because it's simple. This is true because today's computers have something called a graphical user interface, or GUI (pronounced GOO-ee). A GUI makes it possible for you to use a mouse to point and click.

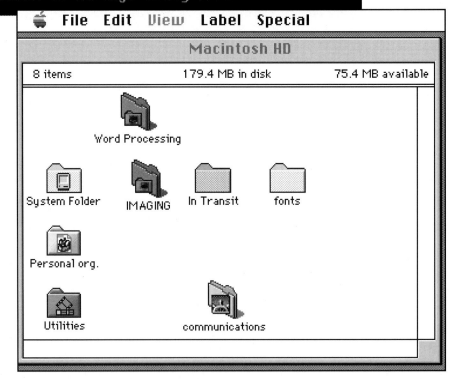

```
Microsoft(R) MS-DOS(R) Version 6.20
         (C)Copyright Microsoft Corp 1981-1993.

C:\HIJAAK>cd\

C:\>mem

Memory Type        Total  =  Used  +  Free
----------------   -----    ------    ------
Conventional        640K      62K     578K
Upper               252K     252K       0K
Reserved            128K     128K       0K
Extended (XMS)   15,364K  14,340K   1,024K
----------------   -----    ------    ------
Total memory     16,384K  14,782K   1,602K

Total under 1 MB    892K     313K     578K

Largest executable program size      578K (592,336 bytes)
Largest free upper memory block        0K      (0 bytes)
MS-DOS is resident in the high memory area.
```

Text inter-faces (left) aren't as easy to use as GUI interfaces (bottom).

File   Edit   View   Label   Special

Macintosh HD

8 items   179.4 MB in disk   75.4 MB available

Word Processing

System Folder   IMAGING   In Transit   fonts

Personal org.

Utilities   communications

18

Suddenly, your computer goes into action. Your message goes zipping over the Information Superhighway to your keypal. E-mail is delivered much faster than regular mail (which some people call "snail-mail").

Letters can take several days to be delivered.

A keypal in another state or even another country usually will receive your e-mail in minutes. That's great news!

Sometimes, however, speed causes problems. If you are not careful, you might write and send angry words to somebody else and later wish you hadn't.

There's another problem with e-mail. When you speak to friends in person, they can see your face. They can watch your gestures. When you talk on the phone, they can hear your voice. They can tell if you are joking or serious. But when you send e-mail, the other person sees only your words.

You can't tell how someone feels by looking at their e-mail.

Sometimes you will write something, and the other person will misunderstand that you are joking. It's easy to misunderstand e-mail because you cannot see the sender's face or hear his or her voice.

Keypals

Exchange e-mail with other kids at:
joinkids@vms.cis.pitt.edu

If someone is angered by e-mail you have sent, they may send you a "flame" (an insult) to get even. Sometimes flames go back and forth. When this happens, it is called a "flame war."

Most of the time, though, messages are understood in the correct way. When there is doubt about how something might be understood, people sometimes use smileys, or "emoticons." They are symbols, or icons, that show emotions. For example, somebody might write the following message to Sam:

Get out of here, Sam : -)

In this case, Sam would know that the message is a joke. (Tilt your head slightly to the left to "read" a smiley.)

Because e-mail is faster than other kinds of writing, it is also less formal. Many people use acronyms to make e-mail even faster. This can be good news—if you understand the acronym. If you don't, it may be bad news because you won't know what is being said. An acronym is an abbreviation that is formed from the first letters of a phrase, such as FYI (For Your Information).

Marine Animals

Write to Sea World at:
sea.world@bev.net

FYI, you can : -)

Smileys (also called "emoticons") use letters and punctuation such as colons, semicolons, periods, and hyphens to send little messages. Smileys help you make sure that people understand what you are saying—if you are joking, or sad, or happy. Here are some smileys and what they mean:

; -) Wink

: - (Frown

: - D Big smile

: - # I'm not saying

: - P Tongue sticking out

: - o "Oh, no!"

: - {#} Smile from a person wearing braces

& : -) Smile from a person with curly hair

Acronyms are abbreviations of longer phrases or words. People use acronyms in e-mail rather than taking the time to type so many words. Here are some acronyms and what they mean:

LOL   Laughing out loud, or lots of laughs

MYOB   Mind your own business

IMO   In my opinion

IMHO   In my humble opinion (often used by someone who does not feel humble)

BTW   By the way

CYA   See ya

FYI   For your information

E-Mail Addresses

An e-mail address looks like alphabet soup. But each letter, word, and symbol helps the mail reach the right person. When you address an e-mail message, be sure that every word and letter in the address is correct. If just a period or a single letter in the

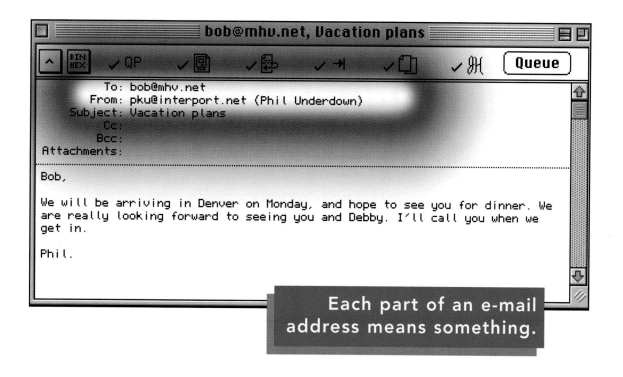

bob@mhv.net, Vacation plans

BIN HEX · QP · · · · Queue

```
          To: bob@mhv.net
        From: pku@interport.net (Phil Underdown)
     Subject: Vacation plans
          Cc:
         Bcc:
 Attachments:
```

Bob,

We will be arriving in Denver on Monday, and hope to see you for dinner. We
are really looking forward to seeing you and Debby. I'll call you when we
get in.

Phil.

Each part of an e-mail
address means something.

e-mail address is wrong,
somebody else might receive
it, or it might "bounce."
When e-mail bounces, it
comes back to you because
the address is incorrect.

Internet addresses are organized by domains. Besides telling you where a person is located, the domain tells you what kind of user the person is—an individual, someone at a school, or someone working for a government. Here are some domain choices:

com	commercial
edu	education
org	organizations
gov	government
mil	military

A typical e-mail address looks like this:

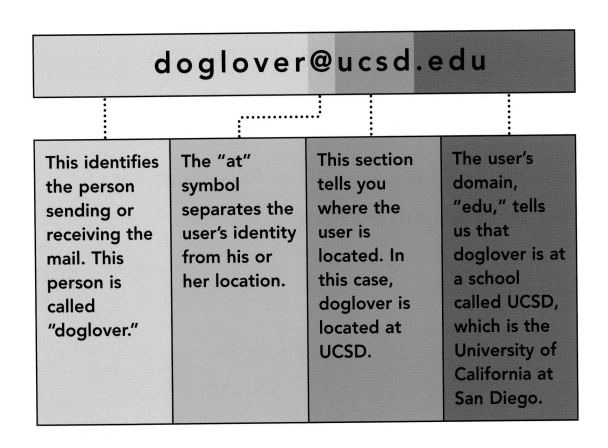

doglover@ucsd.edu			
This identifies the person sending or receiving the mail. This person is called "doglover."	The "at" symbol separates the user's identity from his or her location.	This section tells you where the user is located. In this case, doglover is located at UCSD.	The user's domain, "edu," tells us that doglover is at a school called UCSD, which is the University of California at San Diego.

Two-letter country abbreviations may appear as part of the domain if the user is not from the United States. For example, **ca, au,** or **uk** at the end of an address would indicate Canada, Australia, or the United Kingdom.

Geography

Are mountains growing? Why does California have so many earthquakes? If you have ever wondered about these questions, a geologist can answer them at: Ask-A-Geologist@usgs.gov

Mailing Lists

Some people are interested in baseball. Others want to know about the rain forest. Whatever your interest or hobby, there is probably a mailing list to match it. When you subscribe to a mailing list, you will receive newsy e-mail about that topic. You

Baseball and dinosaurs are two of thousands of subjects covered in mailing lists.

will also be able to let people on the list know your news and opinions by sending them your own e-mail. When you subscribe to a mailing list, you will receive directions that tell you how to send e-mail to the entire list.

To locate a mailing list on a particular topic, you can send e-mail to:

listserv@listserv.net

Leave the subject line blank. Your message should

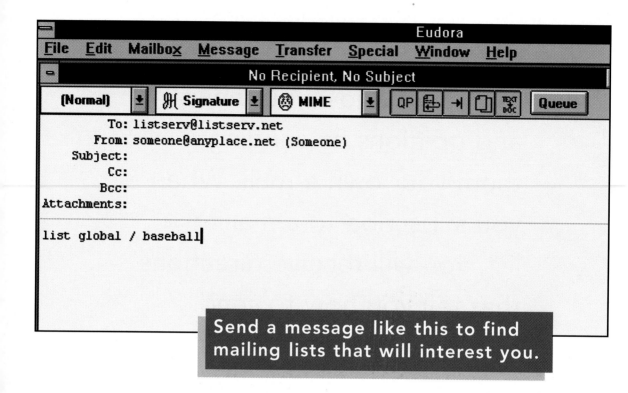

Send a message like this to find mailing lists that will interest you.

state: **list global / topic.**
To find the mailing lists about baseball, for example, your message should state:
list global / baseball.

Mailing lists are a fun way to keep up with your favorite topics. They can also fill up your e-mail box in a hurry, so you might not want to subscribe to too many at one time.

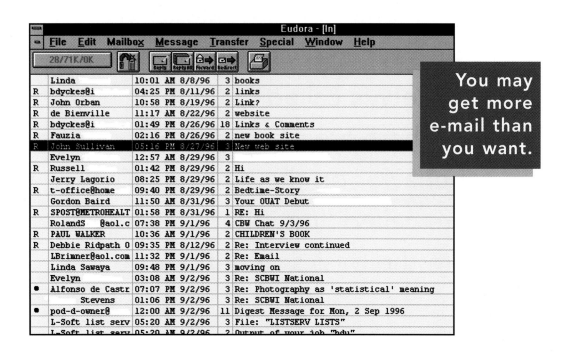

You may get more e-mail than you want.

Netiquette

There are rules for almost everything we do. This is how we manage to get along in society. The way we behave in society is called "etiquette."

There are also rules of behavior on the Internet. They are called "netiquette." Here are the basics of netiquette:

1. DON'T TYPE IN CAPITAL LETTERS. Typing in all capital letters (also called "all caps") means you're shouting, and you don't want people to think you're shouting all the time. Save the capital letters to make a STRONG point.

2. Don't use rude language or call people nasty names.

3. Don't type in **boldface** and don't <u>underline</u> words. Your keypal's computer may not understand.

4. Try to answer your mail as soon as possible.

Always answer your mail!

Safety First

It's fun to exchange e-mail with keypals all over the globe. Most of the people you'll meet on the Internet are nice. But be smart. Bad people sometimes hide out on the Internet, and you may not be able to tell who they are. You should follow these rules when sending e-mail on the Internet:

• Don't give out information about where you live, where you go to school, and what your schedule is.

• Don't give anyone your phone number.

• Don't tell anyone your computer password.

Rainforests

Who can answer your questions about rainforests? Send them to the Rainforest Action Network at:
rainforest@ran.org

Author

Seymour Simon writes books about science. You can send him e-mail at: simonsi@pipeline.com

• If your keypal wants to meet you in person, meet in a public place like a mall. And take an adult with you.

The next time you need to send a message to someone, try e-mail!

To Find Out More

Here are some additional resources to help you learn more about E-Mail:

Books

Internet Sites

Ahmad, Nyla. **CyberSurfer: The OWL Internet Guide for Kids.** 1996. Owl Books.

Brimner, Larry Dane. **The World-Wide Web.** Children's Press, 1997.

Kazunas, Charnan and Thomas. **The Internet for Kids.** Children's Press, 1997.

Schepp, Debra and Brad. **Kidnet: The Kid's Guide to Surfing Through Cyberspace.** HarperCollins, 1995.

International Cool Kids!
http://www.ieighty.net/~ick/
Chat lists, E-Pals, book recommendations for elementary-school kids around the world.

The Internet Public Library Youth Division
http://ipl.sils.umich.edu/youth/HomePage.html
Lots of information about books and libraries. Be sure to visit the Dr. Internet subpage, which includes fun science and math projects, as well as a tour of the Internet designed for kids!

Kidlinks

http://www.intercall.com/ educatio/kids.htm

A web site that provides many links to pages designed specifically for kids

Cyberkids

http://www.cyberkids.com/

Fun, games, and educational activities for kids.

Kids Only

Area on America Online that provides links to such kid-oriented areas as Highlights magazine and Nickelodian on America Online. If you are an AOL subscriber, type keyword: kids.

Larry Dane Brimner's Home Page

http://home.navisoft.com/ brimner/

Learn more about the author of this book and send him e-mail!

Netiquette for Kids

http://volvo.gslis.utexas. edu/~clig/netiquet.html

Advice on how to communicate politely on the net.

Penpal Information

http://www.cochran.com/ theosite/Ksites_part2.html# penpal

Part of Berit's Best Sites for Children, this page lists WWW sites where you can find a keypal.

SafeSurf

http://www.safesurf.com/

Organization that approves Internet sites as safe and appropriate for kids to visit; provides links to many kids' sites.

Yahooligans

http://www.yahooligans. com/

Site maintained by the web browser Yahoo that contains dozens of links to fun and educational web sites for kids.

Important Words

acronym abbreviation formed from the first letters of a phrase; a communication short-cut

domain part of an e-mail address that tells where a user is located and what kind of user the person is

graphical user interface (GUI) makes it possible to use a computer mouse to point and click

modem computer hardware that takes the signals from you computer and sends them over the communication lines

netiquette rules of behavior on the Internet

snail-mail mail that is delivered by a mail carrier rather than electronically

Index

Meet the Author

Larry Dane Brimner, a native of Florida, grew up in Alaska and California. A teacher for twenty years, he now writes full-time for children and is the author of more than forty fiction and nonfiction books for young people, including *Max and Felix* and *Merry Christmas, Old Armadillo*. His other titles for Children's Press include the True Books *Polar Mammals* and *The World-Wide Web* and the Rookie Readers *Brave Mary* and *Firehouse Sal*. Mr. Brimner frequently visits elementary schools throughout the United States to discuss the writing process with young authors, and he makes his home in southwestern Colorado. You can send him e-mail at Lbrimner@aol.com.